My Magical Journalling
ADVENTURES

See it. **Believe** it. **Be** it.

SARAH BENNETT-NASH

AuthorHouse™ UK
1663 Liberty Drive
Bloomington, IN 47403 USA
www.authorhouse.co.uk
UK TFN: 0800 0148641 (Toll Free inside the UK)
UK Local: 02036 956322 (+44 20 3695 6322 from outside the UK)

Because of the dynamic nature of the Internet, any web addresses or links contained in this book may have changed
since publication and may no longer be valid. The views expressed in this work are solely those of the author and do
not necessarily reflect the views of the publisher, and the publisher hereby disclaims any responsibility for them.

Any people depicted in stock imagery provided by Getty Images are models,
and such images are being used for illustrative purposes only.
Certain stock imagery © Getty Images.

This book is printed on acid-free paper.

ISBN: 978-1-6655-9978-8 (sc)
ISBN: 978-1-6655-9977-1 (e)

Print information available on the last page.

Published by AuthorHouse 09/26/2022

authorHOUSE

This journal is for 4-7 year old children. Journalling is a great way to slow down and create peaceful moments to reflect and explore. Your guides are three fairies, Ophelia, Chloë and Athena who will take you through various prompts that will encourage you to reflect on the things in your life that help you become the incredible little human being that you are.

This book is packed full of mindfulness exercises, colouring pages, fun things to think about, do and explore. Each page is designed to help you discover something about yourself or the incredible world around us. We know you will love your Magical Journalling adventures.

Journalling is a gift you can pass forwards. The Dream Catcher Journals make great gifts for your family and friends.

Our mission is to foster more positivity and joy in the world. We want people to **see** their vision, to **believe** in themselves so much that they follow their dreams and **be**-come who they wish to be. Together we can create a world where everyone can realise their dreams and leave the world a better place.

My name is ....

I am .... years old

I love ....

This is your place to shine. The
    magic starts here with you.
  Paint a picture of who you are.

This journal is your magical place where you can dream, create and discover who you want to be.

If you want to, you could even share these enchanting moments with a friend or family member. There's a little note at the back of your journal especially for your guardians.

Journalling is so much fun. Follow your heart, get inspired and see how you can grow your super powers. We want you to use the magical fairy dust you create along the way to sprinkle some positivity around the world. You can share all the things you learn and show your friends how to do journalling too, because if we do this together we can all make a difference and leave the world a better place.

In this journal you are going to meet some magical fairies who will be by your side every step of the way. Alongside you is Ophelia your guider, Chloë the beacon of hope and light, and Athena the inventor. They are fun, spirited and full of endless, magical energy. This is your place where the magic happens, the place where you can imagine and bring your dreams to life. There is nothing in this world that you cannot do, so put your trust in our fairies and let's get going!

Oceans of Emotions

It's magical how many emotions we all have and they all tell us a little bit about us, what's impacting us and what's important in our lives. From jubilant to tragical, exultant to vexed.

We encourage you to talk to your friends, guardians or parents about your emotions and how you are feeling. The way we describe things and the language we use can help others understand how they could help if you are feeling sad or share in a magical moment of happiness.

Be super proud of yourself when you talk about your emotions, especially it feels a little difficult. We have an ocean-sized list of different emotions and they are sometimes hard to cope with, but they are the greatest gifts you can have. One day your emotions will be your signpost to greatness.

Oceans of Emotions

How I feel today

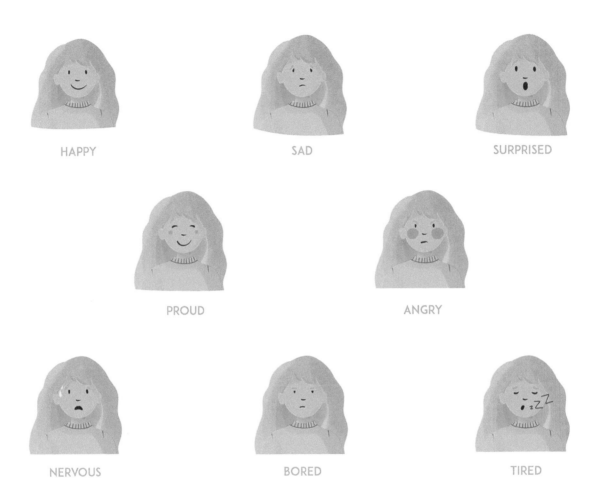

HAPPY

SAD

SURPRISED

PROUD

ANGRY

NERVOUS

BORED

TIRED

Reach for the stars

World of Possibilities

Write your thoughts in Ophelia's balloons below.

You are the creator of your dreams
What are your hopes, your dreams?

Creative Moments

Your hands are your creators. Draw around your hand or paint your hand and put a handprint on this page.

Oceans of Emotions

How I feel today

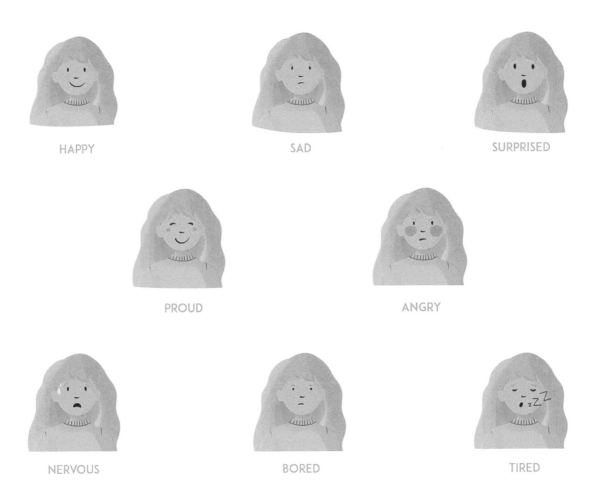

HAPPY

SAD

SURPRISED

PROUD

ANGRY

NERVOUS

BORED

TIRED

Mindfulness Moments

Trace your finger round the breathing star. As you move around the star take a big deep breath for 5 seconds and then breathe out along the next side of the star. Keep going until you reach where you started.

Reach for the stars

I Love Myself

What are the 5 things you love about yourself?

Write them down in Ophelia's balloons.

Be nice to yourself.

I am ...

FUN
KIND
FUNNY
LOYAL FRIEND
CARING
POSITIVE

It's hard to be happy if you are being mean to yourself.

Creative Moments

This is the page of good thoughts.

Smile and draw a picture of some of the fun things that happened this week.

Oceans of Emotions

How I feel today

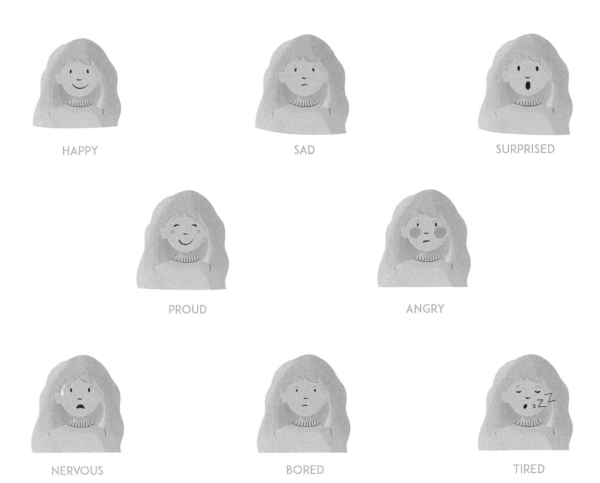

HAPPY   SAD   SURPRISED

PROUD   ANGRY

NERVOUS   BORED   TIRED

Mindfulness Moments

Ask a friend or parent to say 3 lovely things about you and write them down.

Colouring-in Page

Your Super Powers

Write some fun facts about you in Ophelia's balloons below:

1. My superpower is ….
2. I love to ….
3. One thing I do well …
4. One thing I'm very afraid of is…
5. I am a future famous ….

Draw your own super hero.

Oceans of Emotions

How I feel today

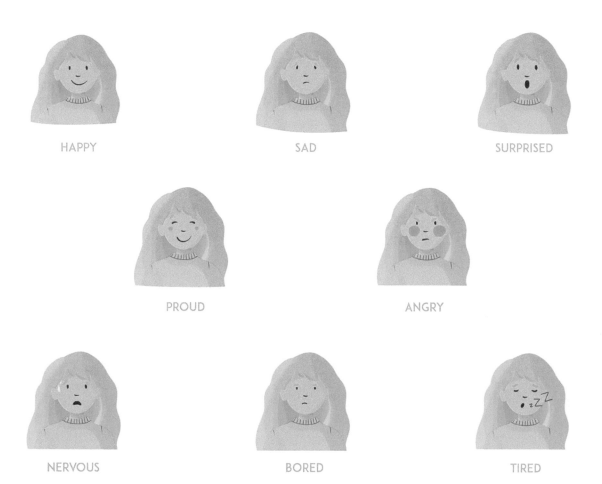

HAPPY

SAD

SURPRISED

PROUD

ANGRY

NERVOUS

BORED

TIRED

Mindfulness Moments

Dragon breathing:
1. Take a deep breath in
2. Breath out your fire with a long, slow exhale
3. If you have paper, watch the paper blow as you breathe out — just hold the paper close to your mouth and watch it fly away as you breathe

Colouring-in Page

Enchanted Fairy Garden

Imagine a magical faraway land and write in the Ophelia's balloons below.

    1. Who would you be?
    2. What would you grow?
    3. The sky would be full of ...
    4. What are you dreaming about?
    5. Who would you invite to your house to play?

Creative Moments

Draw your own enchanted fairy garden.

Rainbow Reflections

How are you feeling today? Write your answers in the clouds below.

Mindfulness Moments

Scavenger hunt

Find a safe place to explore where you can use all your senses, taste, smell, touch and hearing. Write down your answers below.

1. Shhhhhh. Listen and name the one thing that you can hear with your ears
2. Look and name the one thing that sparks your attention
3. Smell and name the one thing that you notice when you breathe in deeply through your nose
4. Describe and name the texture of something that you enjoy feeling (rough, smooth, soft...)
5. Taste and write down what you sense (sweet, salt, sour...)

Happiness

Things that make me magically happy

Write down all the things that make you magically happy in Ophelia's balloons below. Here are some ideas that may make you happy...

SCOOTING

NICE FOOD

MINDFULNESS

HAVING FUN WITH MY FRIENDS

SMILING

LAUGHING

Creative Moments

Draw all the things that make you happy.

Oceans of Emotions

How I feel today

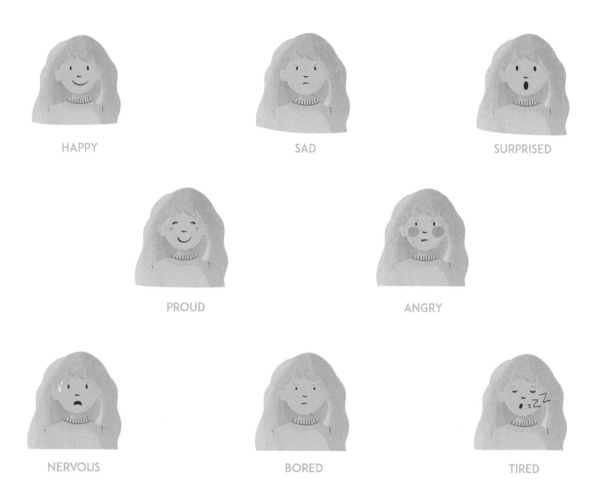

HAPPY

SAD

SURPRISED

PROUD

ANGRY

NERVOUS

BORED

TIRED

Mindfulness Moments

Your mind is made up of all sorts of beautiful thoughts and some bad ones too. Your thoughts in your head are like plants in a garden. There are many beautiful flowers and some worrying weeds that grow. Your mind needs continual focus to keep it flourishing.

So if you focus on the flowers and enjoy planting your seeds for the future you will enjoy your garden. You can choose what to take care of in your garden. What seeds will you grow in your garden? What do you want to learn? Write down your ideas in Chloe's cloud, below.

Gratitude

Write down in Ophelia's balloons below all the things you are super grateful for. It may be that you have a lovely family, a special meal that someone cooked for you, or perhaps that you have had a brilliant day with friends.

What are you thankful for?

Creative Moments

Draw a picture of something that you are really thankful for. Perhaps someone has been kind, helped you or given you a gift.

How I feel today

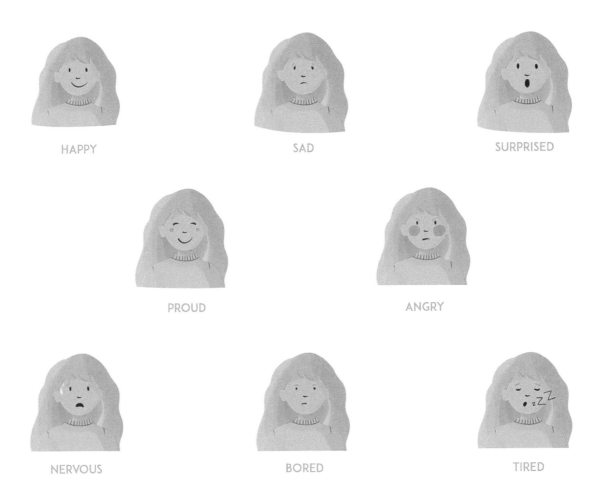

HAPPY   SAD   SURPRISED

PROUD   ANGRY

NERVOUS   BORED   TIRED

Mindfulness Moments

Have you had a wow moment? One of awe, wonder or amazement.

Think back to a time when you felt a sense of awe about something you saw or experienced. Perhaps you saw something special in the garden or your friend did something super kind for you.

Think about how you felt, go back to that moment when you felt awe and write it down.

"Look up, because the best is yet to come."
Sarah Bennett-Nash

Life Changes

Be part of the change you want to see in the world. Write down the changes you would like to make in your life in Ophelia's balloons, below.

Creative Moments

In life, lots of things change. We start a new schools, make new friends or maybe move home. What has changed in your life? Draw a picture of **before** and **after** a change in your life.

Colouring-in Page

How I feel today

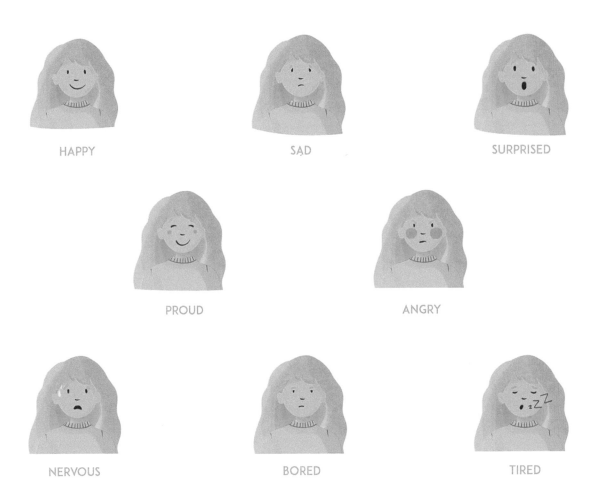

HAPPY

SAD

SURPRISED

PROUD

ANGRY

NERVOUS

BORED

TIRED

Mindfulness Moments

Make your own magical Fairy Garden! Scavenge around your home and find a shallow empty box. Next think about all the magical things that live in a Fairy Garden and then start making your own whimsical setting.

You may have lots of things you've found from beach or forest walks; like pinecones, pebbles, seashells or old buttons. Add them to your box. You can even paint the outside of your box or create a sign for the garden gate. Let your mind wander and your imagination create!

I Can Do Hard Things

Write down in Ophelia's balloons below all the difficult things you've done recently. You may have started a new school, had a new sibling arrive or started swimming.

Creative Moments

Trying new things means you will discover new adventures. Draw a picture of your next great adventure.

Oceans of Emotions

How I feel today

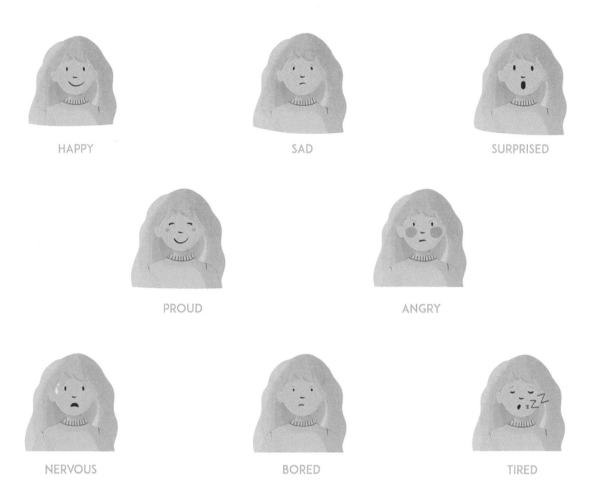

HAPPY

SAD

SURPRISED

PROUD

ANGRY

NERVOUS

BORED

TIRED

Mindfulness Moments

Sometimes we get lost in the forest of worry. Michele McDonald is the brains behind R.A.I.N — a tool for practicing mindfulness. It is so helpful in difficult situations and has four steps:

1. *R*ecognise what is going on
2. *A*llow the experience to be there, just as it is. Don't wish it were somehow different
3. *I*nvestigate with kindness. See how it feels
4. *N*atural awareness. What you are feeling will likely pass soon; it's not forever

Has there been a difficult time in your life where R.A.I.N could have been a helpful tool? Write down your thoughts below.

Colouring-in Page

Calm & Connect

We all get angry, hurt or stressed about things and that's okay. It may be that a friend hurt your feelings or a parent asked you to do something you didn't want to do. It helps to not hang on to these moments for too long and let go of what is making you upset.

Write down in Ophelia's balloons below something that has upset you recently. If you like, you could even cut out this page once you've finished and make a paper aeroplane. Throw it high into the sky and watch your problems fly away!

Creative Moments

What has upset you recently? Draw a picture of those things that have made you angry or hurt.

Oceans of Emotions

How I feel today

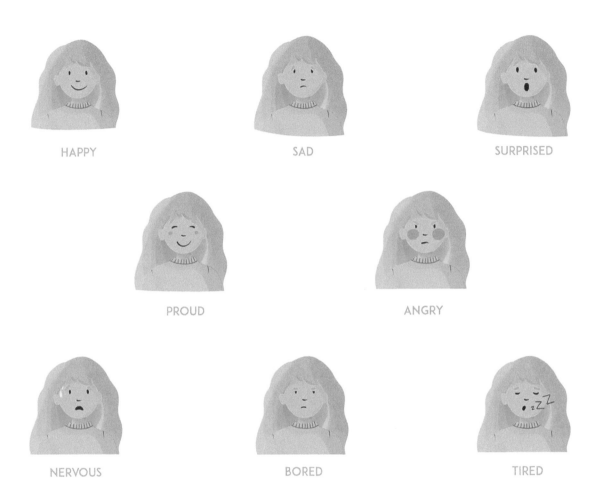

HAPPY   SAD   SURPRISED

PROUD   ANGRY

NERVOUS   BORED   TIRED

Make a calming glitter jar

1. Pour hot water into a jar (not boiling), full approximately 2/3 of the jar
2. Squeeze in your chosen glitter glue and stir until it has combined with the water
3. If you are feeling fancy, you could add 1-2 droplets of food colouring
4. Add 1-2 spoonful(s) of your chosen glitter and mix it up
5. If needed top-up your jar with some warm water
6. Put the lid on and shakey, shakey

Our minds are full of thoughts, swirling around like the glitter in the jar. Sometimes we're sad or angry and our thoughts are hectic like the glitter when the jar has been shaken. It's okay to have these strong thoughts — eventually they will settle down.

When our mind is calmer and less clouded with all the glitter, we can work our problems and make better decisions.

Experiment and Try Something New

Write down in Ophelia's balloons below all the new things you would like to try. Be brave, you can give anything a go!

There is nothing a girl can't do.

Creative Moments

Now's your chance to build a dream. Draw a picture below of some of the things you would like to create, build, be or do.

Rainbow Reflections

Write down below how you could help a friend when they are feeling a little down or blue.

Mindfulness Moments

In the enchanted garden of your mind, think back to the things that you would like to focus on growing. What things do you really want to be good at, and what worries do you need to remove?

Write them down on the page below.

Colouring-in Page

The Wonder of You

Choose which magical super powers that you have or would like to have. Write them down in Ophelia's balloons below.

Creative Moments

Draw your own super hero.

Rainbow Reflections

As we come to the end of our journey together, think about all different ways you have learned to look at yourself.

Close your eyes and think about all the important things you have learned, there are so many wonderful things you can achieve. How can you make a difference in our beautiful world? You may also want to think about someone would like to help, or how you can help them to make a difference.

Building a muscle for kindness and compassion

Think of someone you love, think of something kind and say it to them in your mind. Breathe in, hold, breathe out.

Think of someone you know who is sad or having a hard time. Say something nice to them in your mind that might make them smile. Breathe in, hold, breathe out.

Colouring-in Page

Note for Parents and Guardians

We created this journal as a way of helping children get in touch with their creative self, find fun in activities that will help them discover themselves and reflect on the world around them. It's a space to capture dreams and encourage unbridled creativity, designed to spark the imagination of our little people so they can explore, learn about themselves and start to shape who they wish to become.

I found with my children that journalling together can be such a great bonding experience; chatting about the events of the week and discovering a new understanding of how our little ones think is such a joy. It's also a great way to simply explain the world of the inner self and help to hone skills that will set them up for life.

Talking about emotions with your children is such an important part of social emotional development. Together we can help build an army of little people with social skills like empathy, compassion, kindness and respect. These are tools that will help them cope with the daily challenges of life and when the inevitable stress drops into their path they will able to cope, remain calm and focused and manage themselves. All essential for making good decisions.

Journalling builds self-awareness and skills that will help them become a positive force for good in this world. Positive change starts inside, it's so simple but it can be so powerful. These are baby steps and over time it will help your child build mindfulness muscles. Like anything new, it can be difficult at first to think about what to write and how to put thoughts down on the page. Journalling has so many benefits and has been proven to boost mental health, well-being and social skills. Our journals create a fun space with the structure to help you practice and build life-long skills.

There is so much happening in a little person's life it's easy to miss some of the real magical moments along the way. Journalling is a way of hitting pause and reflecting on the week, the month, or a special event — big or small. It's these moments that are shaping them into the person they are becoming. Capturing these magical moments along the way gives them something special to reflect on in the moment and something to look back on when they are older. It's a relaxed, safe space for you to share together.

We've also thrown in some fantastic mindfulness tools for you to practice together to limit those inevitable explosions! Mindfulness is incredible and can help build skills that foster focus and presence of mind. These habits, formed early on will bring incredible benefits into adult life like being peaceful, kind and compassionate. We are a massive fan of mindfulness at Dream Catcher.

Your child may choose not to share their intimate moments with you, especially as they get older and that's okay. You can enjoy the moment from a distance knowing that they are shaping their thoughts about the person they are becoming. The most important aspect of journalling is that they will be building incredible habits, and a growth mindset that will set them up for the road ahead.

We hope you enjoy this magical experience with your children.

A Little Bit About Us

We are a company that was born out of wanting to inject a little bit of positivity in the world. We create journals and other inspiring products to encourage unbridled creativity. Our mission is to create an army of optimists who follow their dreams and make a difference in the world.

We design products to spark and capture the imagination of people so they can explore, learn about themselves and start to shape who they wish to become.

We want people to grow their ambitions, pioneer their own dreams and create a belief in themselves so big that there is nothing in this world that they cannot do!

Our range of journals will bring a little magical sprinkling of ideas and creations, and empower people to grow their own super powers. We provide a space for people to be creative, and products that bring support and a little joy into the world.

You can find us online at:
Instagram @dreamcatchers.ink
Facebook @dreamcatcher.ink
Website dreamcatcher.ink

A Little Bit About Our Illustrator

Hi!

I'm Jamie, a Zimbabwean-born designer and illustrator based in London. My work tends to be bright, bold and whimsical — a perfect fit for Sarah's vision. Illustration, much like journalling, takes time, patience, and more than a little introspection.

Working on this journal has been such a joyful journey, and I hope that you find the same hope, courage and inspiration on your travels with the fairies as I have found while drawing them for you.

You can find Jamie and her incredible talents at jamiemakes.com.

A little Bit About The Author

Hi There!

I'm Sarah Bennett-Nash and I believe that if you're certain you can make a difference, you will. If you focus on developing every bit of talent, every skill you have, you will start seeing how your choices can drive positive changes in the world.

I'm a public speaker, author, unshakable optimist, wife and Mummy to two gorgeous girls; Chloë and Ophelia.

I turned to journalling when I was having some difficult moments in my life and I've experienced first-hand how it can have a such a huge impact on your sense of happiness and wellbeing. It made a positive and noticeable difference to my life. The power of putting pen to paper and letting the words pour onto the page is magical, motivating and totally inspiring.

I started to imagine how I could pass this magical gift on to my two children. When I started journalling with my eldest daughter Chloë the results were incredible. We shared the intimate moments of her week, the highs and the lows. These are stories she wouldn't usually share with me as we are always doing …doing… doing. Journalling is a great way to hit the pause button, slow down and reflect. I absolutely love that I can help shape incredible habits and a growth mindset that will set her up for life.

If we can all pass forward such an incredible gift to our little people, we will be building an army of optimists who take care of their wellbeing, and prioritise the thoughts that originate from their souls.

The things we think about are what drive us to make the decisions we make, that in turn shapes who we are and who we will become.

Our soul draws on the colour of our thoughts, so let's ensure that we help our little people shape the thoughts that will empower them to stride forth into the world and make a difference.

You can find me at sarahbennettnash.com